Person

Identifying and Maneuvering Around Different Personality Styles

By K.W. Williams

Table of Contents

Introduction

Have you ever met someone that you just couldn't stand? Have you ever had trouble communicating with one person, while you are normally a great communicator and don't seem to have communication issues with anyone else? Do you find that certain people make a lot of sense to you, while others baffle you? Do you like someone, but have no idea how to approach him or her successfully?

If so, then this book is for you.

Everyone in the world is unique. But there are sixteen main personality types that divide people. Most people in the world fall into one of these sixteen categories. Understanding these sixteen personality types and their differences can help you a lot in understanding other people. It can also assist you in getting along and communicating with certain people better, since you know what sets them apart from you. You can anticipate the needs, wants, and preferences of other people, so that you can please them and get them to like you.

This book will help you decode other people. It will remove the complexities and conflictions that you may experience when dealing with other people. With a thorough exploration of personality types and communication styles, this book will show you how people differ and how you can handle those differences. This book will also teach you how to adapt your communication style to fit different people, in order to avoid the miscommunication that makes life so messy and confusing at times.

After reading this book, you will become a much better communicator and friend. You will be able to get along with others better, since you will understand their personalities and what makes them tick. You can communicate and work better with your co-workers, make friends more easily, and generally become a more likable and relatable person once you know how to decode others' personalities.

In addition, you will develop a healthier appreciation for the diversity of humanity, which will help you stop feeling negatively about people who are different from you. Education and understanding is the key to getting over annoyance and your unintentional or intentional discrimination of others. You can easily figure out how you need to adapt your communication so that you can get along with others, which will cut down on the personality clashes that often make interpersonal relations so difficult and confusing. Your easy going, open-minded attitude will attract people and make your relations with others far easier.

You can also decode yourself. Understanding your own personality helps you realize your strengths and limitations. It enables you to figure out what you should do with your life, what you need to work on about yourself, and what types of work or hobbies you enjoy. Knowing about your personality also helps you realize how you relate to others and what difficulties you may run into in relationships with other personality types. You can research your partner's, co-worker's, child's, or friend's personality to get a good idea of the preemptive action that you need to take to avoid conflict.

So begin your journey of understanding and decoding personality types today. Your life will change for the better and you will have this book to thank. Turn to this book whenever you can't figure someone out, or if you run into problems getting things done with a team at work or in class. Happy reading!

Chapter 1: Different Personality Types

There are numerous systems for measuring and determining one's personality. The most common and well-researched is the Myers-Briggs. There is also the Belbin, the Firo-B, and the Big Five. While there are countless other personality assessment methods out there, most of them, such as the Birkman method, require people to fill out lengthy questionnaires. It is not necessary or even feasible to quiz everyone you know. The following three methods of personality assessment are assessments that you can make with your own judgment, so that you can covertly size people up and determine how to handle their personalities in the best way possible. I will go over how to size people up covertly and how to apply that knowledge to necessary scenarios throughout interpersonal relationships in later chapters.

Myers-Briggs

The Myers-Briggs Personality Index is probably the most commonly used personality testing and categorizing system in existence. Carl Jung first conceived the idea of the different personality types covered in the system. Then, in 1943, Katharine Cook Briggs and Isabel Briggs Myers developed a personality questionnaire that effectively sorts people into sixteen different categories of personality traits. While there are various traits that people can possess, almost all people fit into one of sixteen categories. Their social lives, work habits, and learning styles are all influenced strongly by which personality category they fall into.

Each personality type is represented by four letters. The first letter, either E or I, stands for Extrovert or Introvert, respectively. This letter stands for how you get your energy – from being social, or from being alone. The next letter, either N or S, stands for intuitive or sensing, respectively. This refers to how you gather information about your surroundings, either based on your gut or based on the evidence that you are clearly presented with. Thinking or Feeling is what the third letter, T or F, stands for. This shows how one reacts to information and makes decisions in life. Finally, the fourth letter is either J or P, Judging or Perceiving. This is how you use the information that you have learned to lead your life. Judgers live by a standard code of rigid rules, while Perceivers tend to be more flexible and make decisions as they see fit.

If you are curious about what personality type you are, you can find a Myer-Briggs test online. You will find the results very enlightening and probably very accurate as well. Here are basic descriptions of the sixteen personality types:

ENFJ: These guys absolutely love people and want to do what they can for humanity. They dream big, and enlist others as helpers with their charisma and charm. They usually know lots of people and are able to convince people to follow them. They are also experts at organizing people and delegating tasks to people at work. Because they are so social, they are always willing to talk and to meet new people.

ENFP: ENFPs love people. They have great charm and like people, but they also really want to be liked. They strive to be in the spotlight and get recognition for what they do. They are convinced that they are right, and they try to persuade or convince others to adopt their views. They tend to blindly and passionately follow their hearts, and are not great at taking on responsibility. In addition, they tend to collect people and then forget about them as they run along to new friends. They are like excited children, chasing butterflies in the wind.

ENTJ: ENTJs are the ultimate leaders. They naturally fall into positions of high power. They may be warm and friendly as leaders, or they may be cruel dictators and authoritarians. Their plans usually become reality, through their own work and through their skillful delegation of tasks to others. They don't waver; they are decisive and make their decisions based upon logic. Sentiment and emotional frills have no meaning to them; they are simply here to get the job right.

ENTP: ENTPs love to stay busy. They have a million things on their minds and love sharing their ideas with others. Usually they have various hobbies, interests, and even jobs, and they love taking on many roles, belonging to multiple clubs, and always having lots to do. Sometimes they tend to spread themselves too thin and wear themselves out. Some may view them as performers, putting on a constant monologue for the world while not really noticing other people.

ESFJ: The life of the party, ESFJs are generous, boisterous, and social. They will remember every birthday, for instance. They are more than happy to do things for other people, but expect the same in return. If they feel slighted, they will act out; their emotions are big, bright, and on their sleeve. They love to entertain and they easily get themselves into bad situations before pulling themselves out of it.

ESFP: ESFPs believe that life is here for the living. They live large. They like new things and like to distract themselves; they easily get bored and forget about people or things as they spin through life at top speed. They love to entertain, tell jokes, and be in the center of attention, while pursuing new interests avidly and showing off their new gadgets and toys. They also pursue anything interesting, and love telling juicy gossip.

ESTJ: ESTJs like to be part of the herd. They love working with and being around other people. Usually they are followers, who are more than happy to follow the rules set forth by a leader. They find comfort in traditions, rules, and routines and tend to not vary much over the course of their lifetime. They love to do things for other people. But they hate people who are "weird" and don't fit in because they have such exacting standards for what is normal and they don't budge on that. Judgmental but kind, they are content simply being average and avoiding embarrassment.

ESTP: ESTPs are impulsive and competitive. They love to try new things and excel at everything they try. Sometimes vain, these people cannot apologize easily or admit weakness, as it feels like an affront to themselves. They hold themselves to high esteem and dislike being torn down off of their pedestals. They only respect those who somehow beat them or are better than them.

INFJ: INFJs are the best of both worlds: dreamers and doers. They care a lot about humanity because of their empathetic natures, so they often look like extroverts, when in fact they are introverts. They are able to understand others with an almost eerie intuition. Prone to anxiety and mental illness, these people tend to care too much. They are often strong writers.

They are caring and love building teams of people that they determine to treat right. They are also quite intuitive and can spot a liar a hundred yards away. Rescuing others is their strong suit, and also their weakness, as they take on caring for too many people and become depressed when they are unable to help people to the fullest extent.

INFP — INFPs are sensitive and see the good in everyone. They are also creative, sometimes even living in an alternate reality of their own creation. They are introverted, but love people. They become easily conflicted. Usually, they keep their emotions to themselves and like to process alone. Almost always optimistic, they love the world around them and desire to capture it in their art.

INTJ: INTJs are the types who were nerds in school but didn't care because of their dedication to their academics. They are highly intelligent and specialized people who like to be perfect. They often work best independently and like to make their own decisions without checking with management or their spouses first. They will pounce on any opportunity; they are driven and determined. Often they have poor interpersonal skills and focus more on work or academics. Their self-confidence is untouchable once they know something. Their major interpersonal flaw is that they expect logical solutions to romantic problems and they are often very direct and blunt, to the point of coming off as rude.

INTP: INTPs really stand by what they believe in. Usually, though, they stay locked inside their own minds, focused on their own private thoughts. They are very introverted and don't speak to others much, except to perhaps correct poor grammar. They are precise and don't like to waste time chatting. Usually they keep to themselves and they approach social situations in a very dry, removed, practical way.

ISFJ: ISJFs love to serve other people. They like being needed and relied on by others, and they like to fix people. They rarely stick up for themselves and take on too much. They are methodical and accurate, possess phenomenal memories, and work hard. Family means everything to them. They tend to overwork, since they like being needed so much, and so they are prone to sleep problems.

ISTJ: ISTJs keep to themselves...unless a rule is being broken. They have a strict set of personal rules that everyone had better follow, or else. They like consistency and get irritated by others who are less consistent. Instead of using tact, they are usually blunt. They work hard and are dependable. Questioning the rules or the established status quo irritates and distresses them.

ISTP: ISTPs may appear lazy, but really they are conserving their energy. They like mechanical work and using their hands. They are creative in solving problems. They like their space and tend to spread out, disrespecting others' space. Traditions bother them and classroom learning usually fails on them. Instead, they are resourceful and like doing things when they see a clear purpose. In addition, they tend to love wild adventures, trying new things, and being outdoors.

ISFP: These guys are the trendsetters. Creative and living in the present, they are often attracted to the arts. They are highly impulsive and can't stand routine. They will often run away if they feel trapped or stifled. They are both aloof and affectionate, and in fact their moods can rapidly change. They hate classroom learning and need more hands-on, experimental learning. They are easily bored and don't like routines. They need adventure and spice in their lives to feel happy. ISFPs like to do things, rather than write about the things they want to do like their twin, INFPs.

Belbin Team Roles

There are nine team roles that people can fall into. Determining someone's team role helps one determine how a person will perform best at work, and what roles a person would ideally fill in a job. Some people do better with certain types of work than others. The great thing about the Belbin Test is that it can help a person determine if they fit into more than one role, which many people do. People need to work in their ideal roles, however, to be most successful at work. People who are asked to perform roles that they are not strong at may be more prone to failure.

Taking a special test can help you figure out what team role or roles you should fill. You can also use this test on your co-workers and team members to make your team as strong and successful as possible.

Plant

Plants are thinkers. They are creative. If you are seeking an innovative idea or solution, a plant will be able to come up with it for you. Plants are unique in their thinking; they think outside of the box. Unfortunately, plants can be unreliable and can have poor timing, so they need to be managed well.

Resource Investigator

The Resource Investigator is great at finding resources for a team to use at work. He or she will perform research, talk to contacts, and find funding outside of the team to help the team's success. Unfortunately, resource investigators tend to lose steam toward the end of the project and may have difficulties with follow-through. They need to have management that keeps them motivated with reward and that keeps them on-track.

Coordinator

Coordinators are great at delegating tasks between people. They are natural leaders who can step back and see a project from an outside perspective, which allows them to plan ahead and think forward. They also tend to be manipulative and they foist all work onto others, so their power needs to be checked.

Shaper

Shapers love to win and to succeed. Their enthusiasm and drive will keep a team going. They are not afraid to question the status quo and try new things if it means winning in the end. They also are not afraid of change and will push for improvement where it is needed. While they risk becoming domineering and even aggressive, they often provide a team what it needs to succeed.

Monitor Evaluator

These people are great at monitoring the team and making sure that everything is going according to plan. They like to follow the rules and they measure success along exacting standards. For this reason, they can be disliked and they can even be a drag on the team. Their exacting standards and dry logic should be checked by a good manager to make sure that they continue to provide measuring services without dragging the team down.

Teamworker

Team workers love to work in a team. They are diplomatic and they tend to avoid or settle conflicts. Their goal is to understand the task at hand and work well with everyone to get it done. Their only weakness is that they are not good leaders and need leadership to work.

Implementer

Implementers turn ideas into action. They are reliable, efficient, and punctual. Their loyalty is fierce and they always strive to deliver results on a project. Often, they resist change and can pull a team back if they are not kept motivated when change happens. Their inflexibility must be checked so that they do not tear a team off-track.

Completer / Finisher

Completers are perfectionists who need everything to be just so. They will make sure that a project and its results fit the needs of the company. They can be relied on to edit details or to ensure that results are excellent.

Unfortunately, their perfectionism can become a drag to the team, so they need to be given outlets for their exacting standards and obsession with tiny details. They should also be left alone in their work as much as possible, since they know what they are doing and they will do it well.

Specialist

Specialists are experts in a certain field and they focus their attention on the details of a certain science or specialty. They are great at performing research and they also already possess a great deal of knowledge about their specialty of choice. Beyond their specialty, however, they usually possess little knowledge or interest. They are best for specialized, specific tasks that fall within their fields of knowledge.

FIRO-B

"FIRO" is an acronym for Fundamental Interpersonal Relations Orientation. This is another personality assessment which measures one's personality based on three traits, Inclusion, Affection, and Control. This personality assessment is an instrumental way to find out how someone acts toward others and wants others to act toward them. What is great about this model is that it differentiates what one expresses and what one really, truly wants.

This test will indicate how much control one wants over situations in life, and how much control he expresses over the same situations. Similarly, it shows the differences between one's desired and expressed inclusion in social situations, and one's desired and expressed amount of affection from others. A balanced, or transparent, person has fairly even scores between wanted and expressed. A dissatisfied person often desires more than he expresses, while someone who is overcompensating for something will express something more than he wants it. You can find out someone's desired inclusion, control, and affection in order to understand what he really wants, no matter what he says. This is great for figuring out what your partner or friend may want in a relationship, or how your employees wish to be treated.

You can easily determine how people fit into these different trait categories by observing their behavior. Do they demonstrate a lot of affection, yet seem to be very lonely? Does someone avoid participating in activities at work or school, but looks on with longing in his eyes?

Does someone take control of situations, such as having an immaculate home or otherwise being perfect, but is in the middle of divorce? Use these clues to figure out what people really want, regardless of what they portray to the world. Then you can adjust your treatment to give them what they secretly want. This makes people incredibly happy and makes them feel like you "get" them. In this way, you become more popular and you also gain more strong bonds with other people. You can become quite influential in this way.

The Big 5

The newest personality theory holds that there are five major personality dimensions. These dimensions are extraversion, agreeableness, openness, conscientiousness and neuroticism.

Extraversion is how much someone likes to be around other people and their degree of social skills. Some people are more extraverted than others. Watch for how eager someone is to join in social situations. How often does someone speak first or act like the life of the party? Are they more withdrawn? Do they spend their weekends with friends or partying at the club, or do they spend more time at home reading books and practicing music or other introverted pursuits?

Agreeableness is basically traits of kindness, such as altruism and conflict resolution. People who have high agreeableness are easy to get along with, while those with low agreeableness are often aggressive or manipulative. Observe how easily someone reaches an agreement or truce in an argument. Observe if they like to give to charity, or sit around and gossip about everyone. Have you ever noticed them performing any acts of manipulation on others?

Conscientiousness measures someone's attention to detail and level of organization. A conscientious person will usually care about his or her appearance as well as the tidiness of his or her desk, house, and car. He or she will notice things more quickly and will address certain details in work more carefully. Meanwhile, someone who is low in conscientiousness may be messy and may be considered "spacy." Judging someone's punctuality, neatness, and attention to detail can help you make a hiring decision or can help you work out what tasks to entrust certain members of a team with. You don't want to give a spacy person a task that requires a lot of care and attention to detail.

Neuroticism is someone's propensity for mood swings, sadness, and worry. People with high neuroticism are probably prone to anxiety and depression, while those low in it tend to be genial and satisfied with life. You can measure someone's level of neuroticism based on how they respond to stressful events. Do they fly into a panic? Or do they coolly handle their affairs, while keeping a sunny disposition? A neurotic person is not necessarily crazy, despite what the name implies. High levels of neuroticism simply mean that someone tends to be more negative and has a poorer stress response.

Openness refers to how open-minded someone is. A person who is high in openness tends to be very open to abstract thinking and new ideas and adventure, while someone who is low in this trait struggles with abstract ideas and likes traditions and routine. You should judge how open a person is based on how well they react to innovative new ideas or change. If someone always follows the latest trends or has not updated her hairstyle since the 1950s, you can assume that her level of openness is rather low. If someone has a unique personal style or adopts a unique religion, then you can assume that that person is more open and will handle new ideas better. Getting into a debate with someone about new social issues or economic change will not sit well with a person who is not very open, but an open person will embrace these new ideas and changes with gusto and will lean more toward innovation in how society handles the said issues.

You can use these traits to rate people in your mind and find out what they handle well in life situations. For instance, it can be helpful to know if a romantic partner is agreeable and will do nice things for you, or if he is aggressive and manipulative instead. This personality rating can be relevant at work so that you can find out if your customer service agents are good with organization and small details, and if your team members who are working on a new type of computer system are open to creativity and innovation. If you know that someone is high in neuroticism, you can use that information to treat them more delicately and help them cheer up.

Some Things to Keep in Mind

The one thing that makes the above assessment, as well as the others I just covered, difficult is that people react differently in different situations. A person may be low in neuroticism in the office, as she handles stressful deadlines and clients with ease and grace, but she may not be so low in neuroticism in a crowded airport. A person may have the messiest house around, but she is very attentive to detail in her craft and she creates beautiful artwork that is very detailed and intricate. You cannot judge a person wholly upon what you observe in one situation. You must understand that a different rating may be necessary for different situations. Always observe people and try to test their limits to see what they are really made of. This way, you can push your team members at work past their comfort zone and let them grow in their professional fields, and you can encourage your friends to try new things that will help them grow individually.

Another thing to keep in mind about personality is that it stays fairly static over time. However, people do indeed grow and change. Just because someone is an introvert does not mean that he or she cannot grow social skills and become more of a people person over time. Often, it is best to handle people by giving them tasks that their personalities are suited for. They will certainly be successful in tasks that fit their natural strengths and preferences. However, this does not mean that you can never give them tasks or expose them to situations that do not fit their strengths. These new situations can help them grow and develop new skills and strengthen their personality weak spots.

You cannot fully get to know someone's personality just by meeting them once. It takes many exposures to the person in a variety of situations to understand every facet of his or her personality. However, I recommend that you start taking little snapshots of the people in your life as you interact with them. Figure out what their personalities are as best you can. That way, you can learn how to communicate with the person and how to use the person's strengths to make life easier for them. You will find that this makes you a better boss, better friend, and better parent. With time, you will get better at reading people and you will have less trouble determining what someone's personality is right off the bat. Just keep practicing and you will become a very good judge of character in a short period of time.

Chapter 2: How to Determine Someone's Personality

You do not have to be Carl Jung to figure out who people are and how they will likely act based on their personality type. You do not need to know someone's exact personality type to accurately gauge how to act around someone. Simple clues will let you know if someone is more extroverted or introverted, more intuitive or sensing, more thinking or feeling, and more perceiving or judging. You can also guess someone's particular intelligence and communication style based on their speech and the kinds of words that they choose when communicating.

Guessing someone's personality type is quite important. It allows you to determine how to approach and treat someone in the best way possible. As a result, you are able to avoid miscommunication and misunderstandings. You are also able to perform sales or teach necessary information at work or in class in the ideal way. You will find that relations with others become infinitely easier if you take some time to identify their personalities and adjust your actions accordingly.

Here are some tips about how you can read the clues others provide.

Extroverted or Introverted

It is not always possible to tell if someone is extroverted or introverted easily. Extroverts can be quiet or shy, even though they love other people and get their energy from being in social situations. Introverts may be outgoing and may appear to be people persons, even if they prefer to be alone and recharge while alone. So how can you tell which is which?

One way to tell is by speech. Does the person mention how he or she loves to read and spend time alone? Do they have hobbies that call for them to be alone, such as gardening? Or are they more attracted to group activities? This can be a valuable clue.

Another clue is to watch how someone reacts to social situations. At a party, if the person appears to prefer one-on-one conversations or seems at peace just standing in the corner with a drink listening to everyone's conversations, then that person is most likely an introvert. On the other hand, if someone is the life of the party and seems to be having a great time being the center of attention, he or she is likely an extrovert. Introverts can enjoy parties and social situations, but they generally prefer to be out of the limelight.

If someone is stressed or withdrawn in crowds, they are probably more introverted. But an extrovert will thrive in a crowd.

Generally, to gauge someone's level of introversion or extroversion, you need to observe someone's behavior over time. Meeting someone one time usually does not provide an accurate enough picture of their personality. Observe someone over a few times to determine their level of extroversion or introversion.

Once you begin to have an idea of someone's level of introversion or extroversion, you can determine how much social stimulation to give this person. You can also determine if you should give this person space and alone time, or keep them involved in social activities.

Sensing or Intuition

Sensing and intuition refer to how someone gathers information about the world around them. This form of information gathering impacts how a person responds to certain things, and ultimately influences the decisions that he or she makes, which is the third part, or third letter, of the Myers-Briggs personality combination.

People who prefer sensing gather details about the world around them through the physical and real. They infer things based on how people act. They judge people based on their behavior and displayed character. They notice the texture, smells, tastes, colors, and sounds of the world around them. You will be able to tell sensing types because of how vividly they describe the world around them. They also often love to talk about how much they enjoy certain sensations, such as how much they love the feeling of rain on their skin or how much they delight in the taste of chocolate ice cream. These types also tend to fail to look deeper into people, and tend to make decisions based on superficial evidence.

Intuitive people are more abstract. They gather information that is not always apparent to others. They often make assumptions or jump to conclusions that may make no sense to others. Equally as often, they are perfectly right in what they intuit. Intuitive types go off of what their gut tells them. They also are very imaginative and consider the theoretical implications of all of their actions and the potential results of their decisions. These people may deliberate over decisions, or they may make hasty snap decisions based solely on what their gut is telling them. You often won't be able to understand the logic of an intuitive person or how they know the things that they do.

Feeling or Thinking

Feeling people react to life based on how situations or people make them feel. They will make a decision based upon what their heart tells them, rather than on rationality. This can cause feeling types to make decisions that you can't understand. They will say things like, "This just doesn't seem right."

Feeling types also have their own code of morality. They base decisions off of what they feel is right or wrong. They are very conscientious people, who will possibly agree to something and then back out later saying, "I just don't feel good about this."

A feeling person is not necessarily more emotional, though they usually are. A feeling type may be emotionally mature and calm and no more sensitive than the next person. However, he or she still bases his or her decisions off of emotions. Don't assume that a feeling type will be an emotional wreck.

Thinking types make their decisions with logic and reason. They think things through and often take their time, weighing both sides of a decision. They can seem cold at times, as they ignore emotions to do what is best for them rationally. For instance, a feeling type might decide to stay with a cheating spouse because he or she is in love, while a thinking type will end the relationship because he or she perceives that there is a high likelihood of repeated infidelity in the future.

Thinking types don't always care for sentimentality. They are more grounded in the present and don't care about the past. What no longer serves them, no longer matters.

Perceiving or Judging

Perceiving or judging determines how someone prefers to live his or her life.

Perceiving types are often spontaneous. They don't have a set schedule or plan. They don't make lists. They may postpone decisions to find out other options, and they may take their time choosing a romantic partner as they wait for someone better to come along. Sometimes, they make foolish decisions, as they chase butterflies in the wind. However, they are also very adaptive to new situations and they refuse to be tied down by rules or former decisions that no longer apply to them. They are good at letting go of things.

Judging types live by strict rules. Their lives are governed by lists and plans. They hate to waste time and they often make final, executive decisions so that everyone can move on. They have a tendency to be too rigid and judgmental. Also, once their mind is made up about something, they tend to stick to it. Change is hard for them to accept.

How to Determine Someone's Communication Style

Listen to how someone speaks. Do they say things like "Do you hear me?" or "Listen to me closely"? This means that they are more auditory-inclined and you should communicate in a more auditory-oriented manner.

Do they prefer using visual terms? Things like "Do you see?" or "Picture this" or "We don't see eye-to-eye"? This indicates that they are more visually inclined. You should communicate using more visual terms, such as graphs and drawings. Write things down for these people instead of speaking them.

Do they use more tactile terms? These include things like "Do you feel me?" or "Feel what I'm saying." These terms show that a person can learn and communicate better through tactile touch. Use tactile terms and let these people feel things as much as possible. For instance, during a meeting, handouts and tactile tools that these people can actually feel and touch are a good idea to help these people understand what you are trying to communicate.

While it is more uncommon, some people are gustatory communicators. They communicate through taste. It may be difficult to communicate through taste, but you can use more taste terms. You can also offer food along with a meeting or seminar to help these people form a memory association between a flavor and your message. Have meetings over food.

Other people are more prone to communicating in terms of smell. Their style of communication is known as olfactory. You can use scented paper or other scent tactics along with a meeting to help these people commit things to memory by associating the scent you use with your message.

Chapter 3: Communication Differences

One of the major things that divide people is not background, race, ethnicity, religion, or personal beliefs. Rather, it is communication style and preferences. People differ widely in how they communicate. Their personalities often influence their communication significantly.

If you want to decode other people, one of the ways to lift the mystery that surrounds others is to figure out how they communicate. If you figure this out, then you are on a golden path to getting along and avoiding troublesome misunderstandings. You can adjust your communication accordingly so that others understand you, and you stop misunderstanding other people as well. This makes conversation much easier. It also helps you realize things about other people, which evaporates the aura of mystery that some people may appear to have right now.

Communication is indeed influenced by culture. But you do not have to memorize the mannerisms of every culture to be able to figure out the communication style of each person that you may encounter in your lifetime. There are many universal communication styles that different people adopt because of their personalities. Let's go over a few of the major communication styles and the types of personalities that probably use them. You don't have to know much about personality types to be able to tell if someone uses one of these styles, however. You can gather a lot of information about how someone communicates just by observing their speech and gestures over a relatively brief period of time.

Emotional

Emotional people communicate and react to life based on how they feel. They can be unpredictable and unstable, or they can be stable but they tend to be more emotional. While many people assume that women are always emotional in their communication, this is not always necessarily true.

Practical

Practical people tend to be pragmatic in their approach to life. They don't bother with emotions or sentiments. They instead react to life and communicate based on logic and they form their opinions off of data that they receive from their environment. People with perceiving and thinking traits in their Myers-Briggs personality index tend to be the most practical.

Assertive

Assertive people are adamant and clear about what they want. They aren't afraid to speak up for their needs. They also aren't afraid to defend themselves. These people are often mature in their communication and know themselves well. Sometimes assertive people can be overbearing, however. Often, people with the judging trait in their Myers-Briggs personality index are assertive.

Submissive

Submissive people don't stand up for themselves. They would rather let others tell them what to do. They are often agreeable in nature. Submissive types are usually sensing in the Myers-Briggs.

Manipulative

Manipulative people are not direct about what they want. Everything they say and do is part of a larger scheme, to serve an end that you are probably not aware of. These people are indirect and often treat life as a game, wherein other people are the pawns. If you observe someone who is sneaky and underhanded and tends to get his or her way, you can assume that you are dealing with a manipulative type. ENFPs, ENTPs, INTJs, ISFJs, ESFJs, ENFJs, ESTJs, and

INFPs are the most manipulative personality types.

Passive-Aggressive

Passive-aggressive is rather similar to manipulative communication types, but passive-aggressive communicators are not always manipulative. Instead, they use a mixture of manipulation, submission, and aggression to convey what they want. They have trouble being direct and often don't say things directly to your face. They would rather show you how they really feel by pouting or performing spiteful actions. Their insults are often veiled as compliments. Cue the woman who says, "I love your hairstyle. It looks so much better than your old one."

These people tend to be those with perceiving natures, who tend to live their lives according to their perceptions of things, which are sometimes incorrect. They tend to misread situations and then sulk and react passive-aggressively. Feeling types also have a tendency to be more passive-aggressive.

Aggressive

Aggressive communicators tend to use aggression and force to get their way. They use intimidation, threats, yelling, and other threatening behavior to bully people into giving them what they desire. These types can be forces to reckon with, especially when they are determined and really angry. The personality types that often have the most aggression are extroverted individuals with judging and feeling traits. These people are the most determined and tend to become pushy to get their way.

How to Use this Information

When dealing with a manipulative or passive-aggressive communicator, you want to be as direct as possible. Don't let this person get away with twisting your words. It is often best to speak to this through writing or in the presence of others so that you can have proof of what you really said if they try to alter or manipulate your words later on for some devious end. Also, ask these people directly if they have a problem with you. Always use a friendly tone and don't level direct accusations. Simply ask, in front of others, "I heard that you are upset about something that I said/did. My intention was not to offend you. Can I fix this situation for you?" Another tactic is to ask them directly, "How do you feel about this? What do you really want?" Force them to be direct and don't let them get away with their cunning underhanded moves.

It is useless to make emotional appeals to people who are more practical and facts-based. Instead, use logic in your communication and arguments with these people. Convince them about the benefits and rationality of what you are saying. They will take you more seriously if you leave emotion out of your communication with them.

Emotional people are the opposite. You can appeal to them by asking how they feel about things, or telling them that doing a certain thing that you want will provide them with emotional gratification. You can explain things to them in emotional terms. If you want them to come around to your way of thinking, use emotional pleas and describe how you feel.

Aggressive types need to be handled with care. Don't let them bully and intimidate you. Stand up to them, but speak to them calmly and avoid provoking their anger. They don't have to always have their way, but when you tell them no, always explain why in gentle terms and be reasonable. Never be accusatory or aggressive to them, or you will spark a huge conflict. Also don't be submissive toward them or they will never respect you. It is best to look them in the eye while you talk to them; this disarms their intimidation tactics and lets them know that you are someone who stands your ground.

Assertive people are not always aggressive. But they can be difficult to deal with, especially when they have their mind made up about something. Using persuasion and manipulation can disarm these people, but so can making reasonable arguments in your favor to change their minds about things. You should work on being assertive around assertive people. Don't be overly submissive or passive-aggressive, as this will just irritate them and they will push past you, rather than deal with your drama. Generally, treat assertive people with respect and they will do the same for you.

Submissive types are often too submissive and agreeable for their own good. Don't bully these people. Ask them what they really want and observe their body language for clues about what they are not telling you. Don't treat them like they are unworthy of having a say, just because they are more willing to submit and agree to what you want. However, these types take direction well and often make good employees. You can tell them what to do and expect them to do it.

NLP Modal Systems

According to Neuro-Linguistic Programming, a form of understanding of the human brain and how it operates, people also tend to communicate the most using a certain sensory sign, such as auditory or visual. These are known as modal systems. People tend to learn and understand best when information is presented to them using their preferred modal system.

For example, visual people like to see pictures, graphs, or possibly videos to learn. They need visual stimulation to understand something. Being told something may only confuse them. Often they also need to write things down to remember them well.

Auditory people tend to be the opposite. Having something explained out loud is what helps them learn and understand. They may respond well to music or to audio cues. Studying or working with music on often improves their memory and concentration. They will get confused or bored if they are shown something visually.

Tactile people need to be hands-on. Showing a tactile person how to do something and letting them try it once with their own hands will often lead them to greater comprehension than simply showing them or explaining to them verbally. Kids who are tactile learners can learn math using manipulative blocks and sheets, while workers can learn better using hands-on examples.

Olfactory and gustatory communicators are also out there, but they are far more uncommon. They communicate best using smells or flavors. Smell and taste are so related that they are often considered one super sense. Often a combination of both can help someone who communicates this way remember things better. Having a scent in the air when you talk to someone who communicates this way can help them understand and recall what you said better.

Chapter 4: Conflict Resolution per Personality Type

Conflict resolution is perhaps one of the most useful social skills that you can possible possess. You need to know how to settle conflicts and resolve interpersonal issues. If life were perfect, then nobody would ever fight. But that is so rarely the case. You could be the nicest person on Earth yet you will still run into conflicts with other people.

I estimate that probably eighty percent of conflicts that you encounter are the result of misunderstandings. People can be so vastly different in their perspectives and personalities. They come from varied backgrounds, with different cultural influences. As a result, they are bound to interpret things you say and write and even do differently. Some people will understand you; they appear to operate on the same wavelength as you, which is most likely because they share your communication style and possibly come from a similar background as yours as well. But sadly, more often than not, people do not understand what you communicate correctly. They may perceive an insult where there is none intended, or they may do the wrong thing thinking that that is what you asked for. A conflict then appears as you try to sort out the misunderstanding. More often than not, you will not resolve anything because your attempts to clear up the misunderstanding will only yield further misunderstanding.

Even if a conflict is grounded on clashing interests and is not the result of a misunderstanding, resolving the conflict is often easiest if you are able to communicate well. Communication becomes simpler and misunderstandings are avoided when you understand someone's personality and where someone is coming from. You can predict his or her reactions and you can determine his or her needs in the conflict. Then, you are able to propose a reasonable solution that matches what he or she would want. You are also able to communicate in a way that is more effective based on his or her personality type.

Once you figure out what someone's basic personality type is, you have some very valuable and useful information with which you can come up with the ideal conflict resolution. Now let's look at the communication styles different people will use in conflict:

Passive

People who use passive communication struggle to avoid conflict. They may not be happy about something, but they don't want to deal with the conflict that may arise if they try to do something about it. They fail to stand up for themselves or to express what they really want. Sadly, people who use passive communication in conflict often come off as spineless or even weak and pathetic. They do not earn any respect for themselves. But in reality, these people often have revenge plotted for later.

The passive person can be spotted easily. He or she will say a lot of things like, "I don't care, it's up to you." "It makes no difference to me." "Whatever you say." "It doesn't matter to me." "You decide, I'm open to anything." He or she will also shy away from conflict and will disappear for days instead of facing up to someone after a conflict. He or she will never be able to own up to faults and apologize openly. Eventually, he or she may snap because of built-up frustration over never getting his or her way, since he or she never asserts a way.

People who continually use passive communication are often introverted types that may be high in neuroticism. They may also be ISFJs or even ENFPs. Sometimes extroverted types are prone to this type of communication.

The best way to work with a passive person is to actively encourage him or her to speak up. Ask him or her, "Are you really OK with this? Are you sure you don't have anything to add? You know that you can speak here. We value your opinion." Facilitate a feeling of safety where he or she feels that he or she can speak with being greeted by an eruption of dissent.

Aggressive

Aggressive communicators seem to embrace conflict. They have volatile tempers that they are not afraid to express at will. They like to win and they will fight to the bone to get what they want. They often use domination and intimidation to get their way, too. By appearing big and using a loud tone, they often don't have to do much arguing to bulldoze their way into getting what they want.

These people will say things like, "Your idea is stupid." They will insult and demean others to make themselves look superior and to bully other people into giving up the fight. They will also make inappropriate jokes to make other people feel stupid.

If you notice that someone is generally aggressive and loves to win, if you hear them often making insulting jokes or spreading vicious rumors, or if you notice that they seem to take up more room than the average person even though they are not big in physical size, then you know that you are dealing with an aggressive person.

Aggressive people need to be reprimanded. You need to establish that you are the top dog by confronting them and never backing down. Make it apparent that you are not intimidated by them by not flinching or looking down when they try to bully you. When they make aggressive remarks, tell them that such remarks are not OK with you and they better retract their statements. As a boss or manager, you especially need to tone these people down before they take over the workplace and make everyone else miserable. One employee does not get to rule the roost. As a parent, you must punish this behavior in your children and teach them to be kind, or you will raise a child who does not know respect and does not mind bullying others.

Passive-Aggressive

Passive-aggressive people combine both communication methods into an interesting hybrid. Passive-aggressive people also like to avoid conflict, in the vein of passive communicators. But they have an aggressive desire to take control and get their way. They usually do this via means such as manipulation or subtle persuasion.

A passive-aggressive communicator may smile to your face and agree with you. Then, he tells the whole office what he really thinks so that it gets back to you by a third party. A passive-aggressive communicator may also agree to do something for you, but he will sigh, grumble, and act burdened upon as he performs the task to show you that he really didn't want to do it.

Furthermore, watch out for how these people will sting with little verbal barbs, disguised as compliments or kindness. They never express anything directly. Rather, they sneak around with their words and actions, manipulating you into giving in.

Passive-aggressive communication is sometimes very successful. Other times, not so much. If you have to deal with a passive-aggressive person, always confront them about their sly antics. Ask them to their faces, "Is this really what you want? Do you really mean what you're saying?" By doing this, you disable some of their power by showing them that you are onto their tricks. They will realize that their passive-aggressive, underhanded methods do not work with you and that they have been found out.

Now, which of these styles should you use in conflict resolution? The short answer is, none of them. The long answer is, you want to blend different communication styles into one unique and effective style that is sure to eliminate misunderstanding. You want to approach someone very calmly, not aggressively, but you also want to speak up and not be passive. You also don't want to be sneaky and manipulative, but rather you want to be straightforward. This unique form of communication is what I refer to as "conflict resolution communication." You remain calm and collected. You ask people to repeat things back to you to ensure that there is no misunderstanding. You hand out written letters or emails about a topic, and then follow it up with one-on-one discussions to make sure everyone is on the same page as you. You listen to everyone equally and try to work with them, rather than against them, to find a solution that benefits everyone. Doing these things is the surest way to get people to want to resolve their conflicts with you. You are not angering people by being aggressive, undermining the communication process by being passive-aggressive, or ignoring your needs and letting a problem continue without resolution by being passive. You are avoiding all of the common mistakes that people make when they are dealing with conflict incorrectly or at least inefficiently.

In the above sections, I discussed a few ways to handle people who adopt any one of the three communication styles in their communication with you. But let's delve into that a little bit further.

Here a three scenarios that you may encounter:

Aggressive: Someone is very angry. This person is being extremely aggressive in his speech. He is trying to overshadow you with his size to be intimidating. The best way to diffuse the situation and handle the conflict is to first get the angry person to simmer down. You do this by remaining calm; if you respond in anger, you will find that the situation will probably only escalate. Anger tends to grow and escalate until it becomes fury, so you want to avoid that by being a stone wall of serenity. Repeatedly tell the person that you understand why he is upset and that you would love to discuss how you can help him. Don't apologize, and don't engage with him if he continues yelling. Eventually, your calm attitude will spread to him and he will start to become less angry. When he is finally calm, you can ask him how you can help. Carefully listen to him as he states his needs. Then propose what you can do and make it seem like you are working for him. Hide the fact that you are really also looking for your own interests.

Passive: You find out that someone who is usually very quiet on your team at work is acting sullen and seems unhappy. He suddenly flies into an outburst about how no one listens to him or values his opinion. Everyone knows that he never even states his opinions, so they blame him for how he feels. However, blaming him is not the best way to get him to calm down.

Rather, it is better to ask him to speak to you privately. Go to another room, close the door, and ask him to tell you how he feels. He will feel better after he vents to you, and he will also feel a stronger bond to you. Then, encourage him to tell you what he really wants for the team and try to find a way to work his needs into the team's plan. Let him know that he is welcome to come to you and state his opinion if he doesn't feel comfortable talking to the whole team. Ask him to please think about sharing his opinions and offering his input to the entire team, however. "You are a valuable part of the team and we need your input as well. What you have to say matters. If you start speaking up, we can understand what you need from the team and what you think is best. Then we can take your ideas into consideration. If you don't speak up, we can't use your input, and that makes you feel left out of all considerations. Please understand that we do want to hear from you and your ideas won't be shot down immediately as you may fear." A short speech like this can let him know that his passive style of communication is not helpful for anyone, especially him, without sounding accusatory and putting him on the defensive. Remember, using any sort of accusatory language will immediately put someone on the defensive, and hence your chances at conflict resolution are shot.

Here's another passive scenario. Two workers don't get along. One never speaks up but it's clear that he feels unvalued and frustrated with the other co-worker. It is best to pull them aside and facilitate conflict resolution between them. Start by asking the more passive co-worker why he feels frustrated. Let him speak his piece, and don't let the other co-worker interrupt at any point. Then, let the more outspoken co-worker have a chance to speak. Then ask them, "How do you think you two can work things out to get along and work together more peacefully?" This makes both people consider options they have for better communication. It also will get them to calm down and approach their differences from a problem-solving perspective.

Passive-Aggressive: When you notice someone is behaving passive-aggressively, you don't have to tolerate it. But calling the person out will only make him or her resentful and defensive. So, let's say you have a family member named Suzie who is very passive-aggressive and likes to start drama in the family to get her way. One day, she agrees that Disney is a great destination for your entire family to go to on your next summer vacation, but then she complains to everyone else that Disney is for little kids and she would prefer to go to Las Vegas. She complains that you never listen to her and that her wants are never considered. She even brings up old drama, such as how you left her out at your wedding, in order to stir up anger and garner sympathy from other family members. Pretty soon, you are getting calls from all of your aunts and cousins letting you know that you are a terrible person for how you treat Suzie.

At the next family gathering, say in front of everyone, "Hey, Suzie, I heard that you have a problem with how I have left you out of the decision making process for where we're going on summer vacation. While I do feel that Disney will be more fun for the entire family, I think Vegas would be great too. Perhaps we can plan another trip to Las Vegas, or you could go there instead of Disney yourself this summer." Call the passive-aggressive person out in front of everyone, but do it in such a friendly and polite way that the passive-aggressive person won't feel attacked. By confronting her in a friendly manner in front of everyone, you force her to communicate with you openly about her feelings, rather than letting her continue to indirectly manipulate you and others. You also show everyone that you are not the bad guy in the situation.

Take Personality Types into Consideration

If you have an idea of what someone's personality type is, you can understand how likely this person is to be aggressive, passive, or passive-aggressive. Extroverted people tend to be more aggressive, while introverts tend to be more passive or passive-aggressive. The level of aggression and openness someone exhibits throughout his daily actions also suggests how he might react to situations.

When you start a difficult conversation with someone that is likely to lead to conflict, be prepared for how aggressive they might become. You may be surprised at times at how well or how poorly someone handles this difficult communication. Always be patient and be ready to diffuse aggression with your own calmness and lack of emotional response. Once conflict arises, use your conflict resolution communication style right off the bat to propose solutions before problems even arise.

Try to consider how something might impact everyone involved. For instance, if you want everyone on your team to perform a presentation to some prospective new clients, consider how public speaking might affect the shyer people on your team. Before a conflict about public speaking can even arise, try handing them roles such as managing the PowerPoint. Give the public speaking role to the most extroverted, outgoing person in the team. Consider team roles when you give out work assignments to make sure that there is no conflict between a person's ideal team role and the assignment you give him or her. For instance, you can use the most creative person as the plant, who will generate ideas, while the most resourceful person in the team can be the resource manager and handle outside contacts and other aspects of the project that require resources.

Keep in mind how some people communicate. If someone is more visual, you might want to show him a PowerPoint or video to illustrate what you are saying, or draw a picture to go along with your speech. Talk with your hands as well. If someone is more auditory, a good talk is often sufficient, or send them an audio file instead of a written email. By communicating with everyone using their unique modal systems, you are effectively eliminating

the possibility of misunderstanding, which often

leads to conflict.

Chapter 5: Seduction per Personality Type

You meet a great guy or gal and want to get him or her to go out with you or sleep with you. But you will find that all people are different. Some people will respond to certain flirting tactics that you employ quite well, while others will not respond at all or will use hostility to shoot you down. It is best to adapt your flirting style to each person that you meet. Seduction works differently for different personalities. You must get to know what someone's basic personality is through simple conversation or even through building a friendship. From there, you can determine how to best go about seducing someone. Here are some tips for seducing the different personality types:

Introverts

An introvert values his or her space and alone time. Showing respect for this is a surefire way to appeal to an introvert. Once you start getting to know an introvert, allow him or her time to spend alone. Also spend quiet time with this introvert, engaging him or her one-on-one. Suggest that you two go on dates that don't involve a lot of other people or social stimulation. For example, asking an introvert to go on a walk in the park with you to admire the stars and talk about life is far more appealing than asking him or her to go to a party or a crowded mall with you.

An introvert will often require you to make the first move. This is not a steadfast rule, but rather a generality. You should let the introvert know that you like him or her. Then the ball is in his or her court. Give the introvert space, and he or she will come to you when he or she feels comfortable. Keep the gates of communication open but don't repeatedly bother an introvert, demanding that he or she spends time with you when he or she would prefer to be alone. Let him or her come to you.

An introvert usually isn't very expressive to others. He or she may be quiet, and even shy. This is not always the case, but usually it is. Even if an introvert is not shy, he or she probably has a lot going on mentally and emotionally that no one sees. He or she is a master at keeping things private. Therefore, if you tell an introvert that you see how intelligent, sophisticated, or creative he or she is and say that you want to see what secretly lies inside his or her mind, then you just probably charmed his or her pants off. Most introverts never hear anything like this. If you express an interest in actually sitting quietly and listening to him or her instead of just talking about yourself like most people do, you just stood out from the masses as someone empathetic and special. The introvert may not let you in right away, but he or she will already feel inclined to get to know you.

Extroverts

Extroverts are the opposite of introverts in that they require other people to give them energy and make them feel complete. Therefore, if you are chasing an extroverted person, you must understand that you will not be the only person that this extrovert talks to. You can expect exclusivity from a relationship, but don't be jealous that your extrovert has lots of other friends. Never pose rules on an extrovert that require him or her to become isolated.

Suggest fun, social events as first dates. Parties, art gallery openings, or the opening night of a new movie is a great way to get an extrovert out. As you get to know this extrovert, try to do a lot of social activities together. If you are an introvert yourself and don't like social activities, then you can spend one-on-one time with an extrovert, but expect him or her to want to go spend time being social with other people rather often.

Let an extrovert speak. Ask him or her lots of involved questions about what he or she is into. Prepare for a barrage of stories about his or her social life and many friends. This is all just part of being with an extrovert. An extrovert loves to talk and will go on for hours. But he or she will probably indicate an interest in you, too, so don't be tight-lipped. Get involved in the conversation. This will stimulate the extrovert's ego and social expectations, leading to him or her feeling a stronger attraction to you. He or she will continue to want to come to you for social stimulation and great conversation.

When you begin pursuing an extrovert, you need to stand out from the crowd. Sometimes extroverts know so many people that individuals tend to blur into the background and they may neglect to pay attention to you without meaning to. You want to repeatedly work to get his or her attention. You can't be shy, or you will probably escape his or her notice.

Intuitive

Intuitive people rely on their guts, and they usually are not wrong. Never lie to an intuitive person who makes decisions off of how he or she feels about a situation or person. He or she will probably very accurately guess when you are lying, and he or she may also come fairly close to guessing the truth. You will gain a lot more affection from an intuitive type if you are honest and open.

Sensing

People who have the sensing trait tend to rely on the things that they observe to make decisions. Therefore, everything that you reveal about yourself, the way you carry yourself, the way you act, and your past all will impact how you appear to a sensing person. If you want to get with a sensing type, then you want to carry yourself with confidence and integrity.

Feeling

Feeling types base most things on how they feel. Emotions are very important to them. So appealing to a feeling type's emotions is your route into his or her heart. You want to use emotional communication. You also want to make him or her feel good with compliments, romantic gestures, and gifts. Be prepared for a feeling type to walk out on you or start fights with you if you start to make him or her feel bad or unwanted. You never want to be insulting or otherwise hurt a feeling type's feelings.

Love notes are one great tactic that you can use to appeal to a feeling type's emotions and sentimentality. You want to present your crush with things that he or she can cherish. Going the extra mile to create a unique and romantic date, such as a candlelit dinner with roses on the table, is also a good way to get into a feeling type's heart.

Thinking

Thinking types are more conservative about their emotions and rely on logic instead. Being emotional and clingy or sentimental will not gain you any favor with a thinking type.

Instead, you want to appeal his or her logic by presenting yourself as the best romantic choice for practical reasons. You want to prove that you have your stuff together and that you are a good match. You don't want to come off like you will create lots of emotional strife and drama down the road.

In addition, you will benefit a lot by stimulating a thinking type's thoughts. Make him or her think about you all of the time by popping in with sweet text messages and making kind gestures, such as bringing him or her lunch at work. Having great conversations about science or work or practical matters will appeal greatly to a thinking type. Sitting and talking about feelings may not appeal to him or her so much.

Perceiving

Perceiving people are fluid in their approach to life. They tend to base their reactions on what they perceive, not according to a formula. Expect some surprises with a perceiving type. Life will never be monotonous with him or her, and he or she will often be unpredictable. You want to present yourself in a kind way and be very clear with your speech. If you happen to miscommunicate or insult him or her, you can expect the perceiving type to react right away, often very negatively. Therefore, try to make sure that you never present him or her with situations that will trigger a negative reaction. Try to talk things over carefully to avoid a misunderstanding. A perceiving type will appreciate your clarity and openness.

Judging

A judging person has a strict formula by which he or she lives. He or she has determined a code that life should follow. Learning this code is essential if you want to be with a judging type. Also, don't expect to change a judging type or make him or her question his or her values and morals. Doing so will only make a judging type uncomfortable. This does not mean that you have to live by your crush's rules. Just respect his or her rules and his or her formula for action.

Take a Myers-Briggs Test Together

You can suggest that you and your crush take a Myers-Briggs personality test together. This is actually a romantic gesture because it shows your interest. It has the added benefit of letting you find out a lot about your partner, so that you can figure out what communication style and what romantic gestures to use for seduction purposes. You can also figure out your compatibility and likely issues that you two will have, though you should never rule out a relationship just because a personality test says you two are not compatible. A lot of people do this with astrological signs, but astrology is not nearly as accurate as a Myers-Briggs test.

Art of Seduction

Robert Greene wrote a book called *The Art of Seduction,* wherein he discusses different types of seducers and their seduction games. Let's break down these nine seducer archetypes and which types of personalities these archetypes will work on best. You have a natural archetype, but you can adapt your archetype to fit the personality that you are attempting to seduce.

The Ideal Lover

The Ideal Lover is a great style because it is a chameleon style. You adapt yourself based on the person to appear like the most appealing, perfect lover imaginable. You share common interests and communication styles with your crush, and you seem to have no real perceptible flaws. You are (or at least you act like you are) willing to do anything for your lover. Some personality types may see through your façade, such as ISTJs and ESTPs. However, if you are a true Ideal Lover, you won't really be putting up a façade because you actually change yourself to fit each person that you fall in love with.

The Dandy

To use The Dandy seduction style, you must be totally self-absorbed. You must act like you are vain and selfish and even bored by the average person. When you talk, you focus on yourself. You have little shame and tons of self-confidence. This style appeals to people who want to fix you or find the good in you, namely idealists. The personalities that you may find that this tactic works best on are ESFPs, who are self-absorbed themselves and won't be able to handle it if you don't show tons of interest. It can also work on INFJs, ISFJs, and ESFJs, who are idealists and big-hearted lovers.

The Natural

If you use this style, then you are frank and bold. You don't play any games. You also don't hide what you really want. You are open about the fact that you are interested in someone and you are clear about what kind of relationship that you want. Nothing is hidden; you are as unpretentious as a child when it comes to seduction. This style works best on people who don't like to waste time and who don't like games, such as ISTJs, ESTJs, INFJs, ENFJs, and ESTPs.

The Coquette

Using the Coquette style usually works better on men than women. The Coquette plays shy, and is hot and cold. You use a roller coaster of emotions to confuse the person you are seducing, ultimately driving him or her crazy. This style does not work well on those who are reliable, practical, or exceedingly perceptive, such as ISTJs, ESTJs, INFJs, and even ESFPs, as these people will get bored and not want to waste their time with hot and cold behavior. However, this can work really well on people who like challenges, such as ESTPs and ISTPs. It can also work on sensitive, loving personality types who will try to win you over, like ISFPs, INFPs, and ISFJs.

The Charmer

You say cute and flattering things. You always wear a smile on your face and do ingratiating things for others. Basically, you become so warm and charming that the people you are seducing can't resist you. You will find that charming men or women is a very good tactic, as long as you use it only on those who are not very astute at reading people. Avoid using this style on extremely perceptive and astute people like ESTJs, ESTPs, and ISTJs.

The Charismatic

The Charismatic seduction archetype involves being magnetic and irresistible. You make witty jokes, you listen to people, and you engage people in conversation. You show an interest in what they have to say, while having interesting things to say yourself. You use your charisma to please and attract people. This style works for all personality types, as it draws people in and makes them feel good about themselves.

The Siren

The Siren is able to seduce people by reading their personalities and figuring out how to appeal to them. If you are this type, then you exude sexual energy and make yourself as attractive as possible sexually. You are a tease, and you use sensual touching, heavy eyelids, sexy perfume or cologne, silk clothing, smirks, sexy yet innocent sighs, and other physical poses to elicit sexual responses in the people that you try to seduce. As a woman, you lean over to expose cleavage when you drop something; as a man, you brush the small of a woman's back, just to excite her. This style of seduction works best with almost all personality types, though some types may not notice subtle moves, such as ESFJs and ESTJs.

The Feminine Enigma

The Feminine Enigma is a female archetype, though some effeminate men can emulate this seduction style as well. You must be an enigma. You must act mysterious and not reveal too much about yourself. In doing so, you create the illusion that you are very special because the people who meet you can't read you, so they put their own interpretations onto who you are. The Feminine Enigma works best for idealist types, such as ISFPs and INFPs. This style can also sometimes work on extroverts who are used to getting people whom they want. By being enigmatic, you can convince an extrovert that you are somehow special and unique and different from the rest, which will pique his or her interest.

The Rake

The Rake is only a male archetype. He is a shameless misogynist and womanizer. Though he is shady, women can't resist his masculinity and his daring. The Rake often juggles many women at once and doesn't care about monogamy or dating rules. He loves sex and isn't afraid to admit that sex is all he is after. The Rake often works best with women who are introverted and probably intuitive types who know that he will hurt them but don't care. You can use The Rake as either a man or a woman by acting as if you don't care about monogamy, being totally confident about who you are, and being open about your voracious sexual appetite.

Chapter 6: Working with Different Intelligences

Personality is not the only thing that makes people different. There are also different intelligences. People think and respond to life's situations in a variety of ways. The patterns that their thinking falls into is known as their intelligence. People work and understand things best in their specific intelligence, though everyone has a little bit of each type of intelligence. There are nine different intelligences, which we will explore here:

Linguistic

These people are good with words. They find the right words to express the right sentiment. They are usually great at both speaking and writing articulately. If someone is always good at expressing him- or herself verbally, then you can appeal to this person's intelligence by giving him or her more communication tasks.

Bodily-Kinesthetic

These people are great at understanding the physical world. They intuitively understand how the human body relates to physical space. They have great depth perception, coordination, and judgment of things like speed, distance, and impact. Giving these people physical jobs is ideal for them. They excel in careers such as coaching, personal training, kinesiology, and teaching martial arts.

Interpersonal

Interpersonal intelligence is the intelligence of how other people think, feel, and act. People with strong interpersonal intelligence are empathetic and intuitive about others. They are usually great people persons and can relate to others easily. These people are great to use for customer service, client relations, or Human Resources. You can tell that someone has this intelligence if they can relate to you well, make friends well, and love to offer sound relationship advice.

Existential

Existential people are often abstract thinkers who like to engage in philosophical thinking about why humans live and die. They can be great philosophers. Any philosophical and deep people that you meet are probably high in existential intelligence. Often these people are easily bored by the banal and mundane, and need to be given tasks that have deep meaning.

Logical-Mathematical

Your typical math geek usually has a very logical, sound mind for reasoning and understands numbers intuitively. People who are great at math are also usually not so great with gramma and linguistics because they use their left brain more than their right. Therefore, don't burden a logical-mathematical person with writing tasks or spend too much writing them long, fancily-worded emails or correcting their grammar.

Musical

If you meet a musician, sound producer, or sound technician, you are talking to someone with high musical intelligence. Almost all people love music, but only some people are actually able to understand rhythm, timing, key, tone, etc. Musically inclined people are often great at working with sound and technology, as well as making music. Encourage the people you know with this intelligence to play musical instruments if they work a job that has nothing to do with music; this will make them feel more content in their lives. Often, if you play music, you can heighten their energy and interest, but you may also distract them from the task at hand because they become obsessed with the beat of the music.

Naturalistic

These people are biologically intelligent. They understand Nature and how life works. They make great doctors, botanists, biologists, zoologists, veterinarians, EMTs, and gardeners or animal keepers. Engage people who seem fascinated by natural life with conversation about how life works, and give them any work tasks that have to do with things like medicine, pharmacology, biology, and zoology. Also, encourage these people to go outside and enjoy Nature. A great date with someone high in this intelligence may be a visit to a zoo or botanical garden, or a tour of a farm.

Spatial

People who are high in spatial intelligence can see the world in 3D. They have an intuitive understanding of space, time, distance, and how the mechanics of different things work. These people can excel in carpentry, construction, physics, engineering, or even art and computer design. Task them with doing PowerPoint presentations for work and designing graphics for the company website. Engage them by having them perform maintenance and repairs around the house or by involving them in figuring out how something like a car works.

Intrapersonal

Intrapersonal intelligence is something that we all have a bit of. It is the understanding of who you are and what you want in life. It is involved introspection that goes deeper than simply understanding that you are hungry. Intrapersonal intelligence is great because people who have high amounts of it are very self-aware and don't easily become confused. They exercise good judgment. Often, they can turn that intrapersonal intelligence outward to understand other people, meaning that high intrapersonal intelligence is often strongly linked with high interpersonal intelligence. These introspective people often indicate their form of intelligence by keeping a journal and talking about what motivates them. You should keep them engaged by giving them tasks that they find meaningful and listening to their input.

Chapter 7: Letting People into Your Life and Choosing Your Friends

One of life's greatest challenges is finding good people to spend time around. Do you want to hang out with people who repeatedly hurt you, manipulate you, and bring you down? Do you want to waste your time trying to communicate with people who just don't "get" you? Or do you want to surround yourself with positive people who uplift you and make you feel good about yourself? If you are ready to become more discerning about who you let into your life and your heart, then read this chapter about picking better friends.

The people that you associate with play a big role in how you feel about yourself. That is why it is so important to pick good friends who treat you well and actually care about you. You want people who encourage you to be your best self, and who project confidence and good habits onto you. You also want to solidify and improve your reputation by appearing with good people who don't behave like children. Therefore, it is essential that you begin to pick better friends.

It is relatively easy to observe someone's behavior and make a decision about whether or not that person is good for you to be around. For example, if someone gossips a lot, you can surmise that he or she will probably talk about you behind your back too, so you can decide not to befriend that person. If someone is helpful and caring, bringing care baskets to sick friends and volunteering for charities, you can assume that that person will probably at least try to be a good friend to you. Avoid drug addicts, people who don't take care of themselves, and people who are mean, spiteful, or vindictive. Observe people for a while before you actively befriend them. You usually don't have to watch people for very long before you start to notice their primary behavior. Don't be shy about rejecting people who are not healthy, who have tons of life problems that they blame on others, who manipulate people, who don't care for themselves, or who have mean traits or bad habits. These people are toxic and will just drag you down.

Go for people that reflect what you want out of your life. These people are aligned with your goals and will encourage you by example.

For instance, if you want to become a career person, then hang out with entrepreneurs and people who have successful careers. If you want to get healthy, join a gym and hang out with other fitness junkies and health food cooks. Do the activities that you enjoy so that you can meet people who share your interests and your passions, as well. These people will encourage you to be who you want to be and will push you to be a better person. They will fuel your passions and interests and prevent you from falling into stasis in life.

It is OK to let go of old friends. Sentiment does not mean very much in the long run. If someone has been your friend for years, but keeps you in a life that you don't want anymore, then go ahead and discard that person. He or she no longer serves you well. You can maintain a relationship if you really don't want to cut a person out of your life or feel wrong for saying good-bye, but keep distance so that this person doesn't taint your life with the things that you now want to move on from.

Now let's look at personalities. If you take a personality quiz, you can find out what personality type you are. From there, you can find out what other personality types you are compatible with. But I disagree with using compatibility as a means to find friends. Yes, you are more compatible with some personalities than others, but that does not mean that you cannot find a really great friend in an unexpected or incompatible personality type. If you two are strong enough to work through your differences and make it work, then your relationship is probably even stronger than your relationships are with people that you just naturally get along with. Testing your comfort levels and exploring the diverse types of people in this world is a good thing. It keeps you from falling into a rut and it opens you to lovely and delightful experiences.

You can use compatibility to determine what problems you may run into with someone, such as a future romantic partner. Figure out what clashes you are likely to have so that you can work through those issues more efficiently. But don't use personality compatibility to match you with people or to decide against befriending or dating someone. That just limits you unnecessarily and can kill your chances of a beautiful relationship.

When it comes to choosing who to let into your life using personality, here are some guidelines that you can follow. But never use these guidelines as steadfast rules. Consider that there are always exceptions.

Fun People

If you want a friend who is entertaining, adventurous, and generally just fun to be around, then go for people who are ISTPs, ISFPs, ESTPs, ENFPs, and ESFPs. ISFPs are generally zany and creative people who may keep to themselves, but reveal a whole other side when you get to know them. ISTPs are people who love to experiment, try new things, and boldly advance into new territory. ESTPs are the most likely to be entrepreneurs, and they are great people persons who love trying new things and aren't afraid to be themselves. ESFPs are entertainers who are never boring, and are usually involved in things like acting, theatre, and other forms of performing and entertaining. They often throw the best parties, and have lots of other eclectic friends. ENTPs love intellectual debates and vivid conversations.

Career-Minded People

If you want to hang out with people who are more focused on career and goal satisfaction, then hang out with ESTPs, who are the most likely of all personalities to start their own businesses. Or hang out with ESTJs, ENTJs, or ENFJs, who like administration roles and positions of power and are often natural leaders. ENFPs are enthusiastic and creative, and often driven to work with others toward making their dreams and goals reality. They also are most likely to have lots of connections for you to expand your business and social network with. INFPs are often also career-driven, but they are more introverted and tend to not be very social when they are focused on work.

Caring People

Sometimes you just want a loving, caring friend. The types who are most likely to be warm and caring include ISFJs and ESFJs. ESFPs are also extremely charming and social, as are ENFPs. These personality types love people, defend their loved ones fiercely, and make wonderful friends. This is not to say that you can't find a warm, caring friend in other personalities, but these four are the most outgoing and loving of all.

Positivity and Enthusiasm

Are you seeking someone who is enthusiastic and driven? Well look no further than ENTJs, ENFPs, ESFJs, ISFJs, ISFPs, ESTPs, and ESFPs. ISTPs and ISTJs are often passionate about their fields or specific hobbies as well, though they may not care for much else.

Popular People

If you want to make more friends, but you are a bit of an introvert or you are new to an area or you don't get out much, then pair up with a huge extrovert. Extroverts tend to have lots of friends. Ask your extroverted friend to introduce you to some new people, as well. From there, you will meet new people and be able to network more efficiently. Some of the most popular people are usually ENFPs, ESFJs, and ESFPs.

Also, reach out to introverts, who often want more friends. Be the first person to start a conversation and make the introvert feel like his or her input is highly valued. This will make you quite popular with anyone that you talk to, but especially introverted types will appreciate your engagement.

Chapter 8: Accepting Yourself and Others

You have your own unique personality. No matter what you tested as on the Myers-Briggs scale or any other personality assessment scale, you know who you are inside. You are a unique soul who is not like anyone else. Your very existence is so original that it is a special gift to the world. Embracing who you are and loving yourself is so important for your health and happiness.

You really cannot change yourself very much, so it is better to accept yourself and work with what you have. You have all of the tools necessary to be successful in life, so use them. Take advantage of your strengths. View your weaknesses not as flaws, but as areas that you can work on in life.

Many introverts wish that they could be extroverts. If you are an introvert, you need to accept that about yourself. You will never be able to become an extrovert. As an introvert, you are still wonderful; you also have special gifts to give to the world, such as introspection and creativity and independence. And just because you are introverted does not mean that you cannot develop your social skills and become a more people-oriented person.

If you are more sensitive than you would like to be, that can feel like a curse. But sensitivity and empathy are actually quite rare in this world. Someone out there has benefited from your sensitivity. Preserve this trait and understand that you hold a rare gift, even if the rest of the world does not seem to appreciate it.

If you are a more aggressive person, channel that aggression into something healthy, such as business or sports. You can use your aggressive communication style to drive a hard bargain and never back down. That is a valuable quality. If, on the other hand, you are a passive person, also accept that as a gift. You can use your passivity for a variety of jobs, including the healing professions. You can also work on standing up for yourself, standing your ground, and speaking up when your opinion is asked for. You don't have to take life lying down.

There are a million other examples of traits that you may hate about yourself. Understand that you are designed to be a certain way for a reason. You have positive traits and you offer the world great value just as you are. If you don't like something about yourself, you are more than welcome to change it, but don't hate yourself because of this one flaw or trait.

One benefit to finding out more about your personality is that you can understand your strengths and weaknesses better. In the past, you may have been bullied or you may have beaten yourself up because you did not have certain social abilities or you weren't good at certain jobs. Now, you can see why that is, and you can pinpoint areas of weakness where you can build yourself up. You can use personality assessments to gain a more thorough self-awareness and to stop blaming yourself for not being like everyone else. Everyone is different and you have your specific strengths and weaknesses. Instead of beating yourself up over that, use that information to understand yourself better and put yourself in positions and situations where you are more likely to be successful in the long run. Use your personality type to find jobs that you can excel at, and to figure out what you need to work on inside yourself.

Another benefit is that you can determine where you stand in relation to others. For instance, if you measure more of a sensing type than an intuitive type, then you can gather that you judge others based off of the information that you gather from them, not based off your gut instincts. Therefore, you can work on becoming more astute at reading people by picking out the right information and not letting appearances or what people say deceive you. If you are a more extroverted type and can't stand being alone, you can focus on developing a network of healthy people to draw your energy from. You can use personality index information to improve your life and your interpersonal relations.

Never should you take the results of a personality assessment and let them rule your life. Just because you are an INFP, for example, doesn't mean that you should only go after jobs such as writing and editing, where you don't have to be very social. Don't limit yourself based on the results of your assessment. You should accept yourself as you are, but don't limit yourself because you think that your personality type is all that you are. As a human being, you are complex. You go beyond the simple algorithm that makes up your personality type. Your personality type will probably aptly describe you and provide a good guide for the kinds of jobs that you will excel at, but if you really love something, you should do it no matter what your personality index tells you. Grow as a person and build up your weaknesses by taking on jobs and tasks that go beyond what your personality type says your strengths are. Back to the INFP example, many people told me that I could never become a cosmetologist because I am naturally introverted. But I surprised everyone, including myself, by going after what I loved. Now I am a successful cosmetologist even though I am an introverted individual.

Accepting other people as they are can also be a special challenge. There are people out there that you may just want to have disappear. Some people are very difficult for you to get along with and communicate with. But the diversity of humanity is beautiful. Accepting the fact that other people are the way that they are is the first step that you can take toward a more peaceful coexistence with others. If you continue to refuse to accept other people who are different than you, then you will be very lonely and often very frustrated.

Instead, embrace people for how they are. Embrace the fact that they look at things and do things differently than you. Understand that they have their strengths and places in life where they excel. You have your place. You all ultimately must work together to create a wonderful existence on Earth. Since everyone offers the world value, each person is simply one part of a huge, colorful, diverse mosaic.

There are people out there that your personality is bound to clash with. Ego conflicts are a normal part of the human existence. You are better off just avoiding people who cannot seem to work well with you. You don't need to waste your time fighting with people who refuse to respect you and work with you. However, realize that you cannot change these people and that hating them is not helpful either. Just take the high road and move on.

Some personality types are more manipulative than others. Some people are just naturally good at manipulation, and they realize that it is the easiest and fastest way to get what they want. It is best to also avoid these people. But accept that they have found a benefit from being manipulative, so they cannot be changed. You have every right to protect yourself from being manipulated. This does not mean that you should engage in fighting with a manipulative person. Just accept them and move on, as well.

When you become more accepting of others and their differences from you, you naturally put your guard down. You also begin to understand that some people have weaknesses and strengths that you don't have, and you realize that everyone has some sort of intrinsic value. You will be surprised at how easily other people pick up on this new attitude of yours. Suddenly, if you start accepting people as they are and trying to work with them instead of against them, you will notice that people like you more. Your interactions with other people become much simpler and pleasanter. You will encounter far less conflict as your days go by. The information in this book can help you decode people and understand them better, so that you can open your heart and begin the road to acceptance of everyone. It will also help you react and act better toward people based on their personalities, which will make life easier for you.

Conclusion

No one quite knows what creates personality. There are theories that personality is dictated by genes, or molded by background and upbringing. What is interesting is that despite the diversity of the world and humanity, almost all people fit into one of sixteen categories. People also tend to fall into the same range on spectrums measuring control, inclusion, openness, extroversion, and aggression. So while people are different, there are many people who are very similar who belong to the same personality categories.

Reading people can be different. But now that you have read this book, you understand how to read people more thoroughly and accurately. Now you can observe people over a short period of time and realize how they will react to situations, how to handle conflict with them, and what appeals to them most. You can also figure out what roles to assign your co-workers or employees in a team to make sure that everyone is happy and successful at their jobs. The more you practice this character reading, the more proficient you will become at it, until you are able to read people after one brief meeting.

Knowing how to read someone's personality basically allows you to decode the person. You can figure out all sorts of useful information that enables you to work things out with them and communicate with them well. You can use personality as a means to figure out how to communicate, seduce, resolve conflict, and make friends with someone. You can also use it as a way to find better friends and improve the quality of people that you associate with.

No matter what your personality is, you can adapt your communication style to get along with anyone and everyone. You no longer will find that there are some people that you just hate or can't seem to communicate with. You can adapt to get along with everyone and to handle conflicts with even the most aggressive, unreasonable people. Your life will benefit greatly from your ability to get along with everyone harmoniously. With this ability comes great peace and success. The secret in your back pocket is purely communication. You now know how to read people, figure out what their communication style is, determine what their needs are based on their personality type, and thus how to please them and resolve conflict with them appropriately.

A lot of people will start to get along better with you. And you will begin to appreciate all people, no matter what their personality is. You will also learn to love yourself, as you begin to understand that you are not a flawed human being but instead have weaknesses and strengths that balance each other out. Start living your life utilizing your strengths, building up your weaknesses, and loving yourself as you are.

Other books available by K.W. Williams on Kindle, paperback and audio

Lifting The Clouds: How To Support A Loved One With Depression

Meditation 101: Beat the Stress with the Power of Your Mind

The Science of Self Massage: Independently Relieve Stress Using Techniques That Target Trigger Points

Made in the USA
Middletown, DE
15 January 2018